CREEPY SPOOKY SCIENCE

Sandra Markle
Illustrated by Cecile Schoberle

Hyperion Paperbacks for Children
New York

First Hyperion Paperback edition 1996

Printed in the United States of America.

1 3 5 7 9 10 8 6 4 2

The text for this book is set in 11-point Candida.
Designed by Lara S. Demberg.

Library of Congress Cataloging-in-Publication Data

Markle, Sandra.
Creepy, spooky science / Sandra Markle ; illustrated by Cecile Schoberle.
p.   cm.
Summary: Presents an assortment of awesome experiments with
information about the scientific principles involved.
ISBN 0-7868-1088-2 (pbk.)—ISBN 0-7868-2178-7 (lib. bdg.)
1. Science—Experiments—Juvenile literature.   2. Scientific
recreations—Juvenile literature.   [1. Science—Miscellanea.
2. Science—Experiments.   3. Experiments.]   I. Schoberle, Cecile, ill.
II. Title.
Q164.M27   1996
507'.8—dc20   95-50780

TABLE OF CONTENTS

This book is guaranteed to have you quivering over science—for real! And don't bother to wash your hands before you start experimenting. You'll soon be whipping up a recipe for blood and planting seeds in the dark. You'll be peeking at your own bones, too, and creating some very creepy sounds. If that's not enough to give you goose bumps, you'll also discover how a body is embalmed to keep it from decomposing, and you'll practice some embalming strategies of your own. Then there's still more creepy, spooky stuff—all for the sake of science.

You'll need materials you can find at home or buy cheaply at a grocery store, gardening store, or hardware store. Along the way you'll also have opportunities to develop your own experiments. How spooky and disgusting you make them is up to you, providing you first check out your plans with an adult. But to help you get started, here are steps you can work through to tackle any problem-solving situation:

1) Think about everything you already know about the problem. What did you learn by doing an earlier investigation? Is there anything you could look up if you visited the library?

2) Brainstorm possible solutions. Limit yourself to no more than fifteen minutes and write down every idea that comes into your head.

3) Analyze your list of possible solutions. Be critical as you consider reasons why your ideas might not work. Choose the one idea you think you have the

best chance of being able to use successfully. Be sure to check with an adult that what you want to try will be safe for you.

4) Test your solution. If you are setting up an experiment, be sure that everything is identical except the one thing you want to change. For example, in the activity on page 65, you'll be using salt to float an egg in water. Everything about the test should be identical except for the amount of salt used. Every test should also be repeated at least three times to be sure the results are what is likely to happen every time.

5) Always analyze the results of your test. Did your idea work? From what you discovered, is there anything else you could try that might work even better?

Remember

- Don't do any activity that requires you to use a stove or a microwave without an adult partner.
- Clean up the work area after you finish your activity.
- Recycle materials whenever possible.
- Have fun!

Okay. Don't get comfortable. It's time for spooky action! Some of these investigations will be done in the dark, so grab a flashlight to read the directions. Then brace yourself for the spine-tingling activities ahead and turn the page to get started!

Pour a Glassful of Vampire Blood

Are you brave enough to pour a glass of blood? If so, try this.

You'll need:
- **6 laxative tablets that contain phenolphthalein (available at grocery stores and drugstores)**
  *Note: The chocolate-flavored kind will not work.
- **measuring spoon**
- **measuring cup**
- **self-sealing plastic bag**
- **hammer or rock**
- **cutting board**
- **clear glass**
- **powdered dishwasher soap (any brand)**

Put the six laxative tablets in the bag. Seal the bag and put it on the cutting board. Use the hammer or rock to crush the tablets into a powder. Dump the powder into the glass. Now add a teaspoon of the powdered dishwasher soap and pour in a cup of water.

Eeeeeeeeeek! Suddenly, the glass looks like it's full of bright, purplish red liquid—vampire blood. But don't panic. This is just a trick. The phenolphthalein is a special kind of chemical called an *indicator*. Indicators are substances that change in a way that lets you easily tell when a certain kind of a reaction has taken place. What's really happening here is that the normal molecular structure of phenolphthalein makes it reflect all light so you see it as white or colorless. But when it comes in contact with another kind of substance, called a *base*, this molecular structure changes. You'll find bases such as sodium carbonate, sodium sulfate, or other related chemicals listed with the ingredients on the dish-washing-soap package. When its molecular structure changes, the phenolphthalein absorbs some light, and you see a color—pink. The stronger the base, the brighter the shade of pink.

Now you're probably wondering what a base is. It's

one of two important groups of chemicals called *acids* and bases. These are found everywhere around you— even inside you. There's hydrochloric acid produced naturally in your stomach to help break down the food you eat. Other acids such as sulfuric acid are used in car batteries and to make plastics and fertilizers. There are also acids in many foods, such as lemons and oranges. It's the acid that gives these foods their sharp taste. Bases are chemicals that can dissolve fats and oils. So bases are used in cleansers, such as dishwashing soap, and in deodorants. Baking soda is one of the few bases you can eat. It's an important ingredient in many recipes.

Don't throw the vampire's blood away. You'll need it for the next activity.

Make the Blood Boil

Get ready to see something really wild. You're going to make the glass of vampire's blood bubble and foam, just as if it were boiling.

You'll need:
- **measuring spoon**
- **vinegar**
- **baking soda**

Set the glass of vampire's blood in the sink. Pour in a tablespoon of baking soda. Add a tablespoon of vinegar and watch what happens. The liquid starts to bubble and foam, just as if it were boiling. But touch the outside of the glass and you'll discover that it's not hot. In fact, you're witnessing a *chemical reaction*.

Dr. Timothy Wilson, postdoctoral student in organic chemistry at Georgia Institute of Technology, explained that when the vinegar (acid) and baking soda (base) react, the molecular structure of both substances breaks down. Then hydrogen is released, creating bubbles. Oxygen and carbon are released, too, and combine, forming carbon dioxide, which also produces bubbles. There's no way to tell which bubbles are hydrogen and which are carbon dioxide just by looking at the froth, but the effect *is* impressive.

Creepy Cool!

Spooky Juice Sleuth

Ready for some more colorful chemical fun? Then perform this experiment, using grape juice to find out which mystery liquid is an acid and which is a base.

You'll need:
- **100 percent real grape juice**
- **measuring spoon**
- **4 glasses or clear plastic cups**
- **vinegar**
- **lemon juice**
- **ammonia**
- **measuring cup**
- **safety goggles**

You'll be using ammonia, which is a strong chemical, so to stay safe, wear safety goggles, work with an adult partner, and follow the directions carefully.

There's a mystery base lurking among the liquids you've collected. Is it the lemon juice, the vinegar, or the ammonia? Guess.
(Remember, bases are often used as ingredients in cleansers.)
   To find out if you're right, follow these steps:
1) Mix up the grape-juice solution in a glass by adding one part juice to nine parts water. For example, add

6

one tablespoon of grape juice for every nine table-spoons of water.

2) Set three glasses in a row. Pour 1/4 cup of lemon juice into the first glass, 1/4 cup of vinegar into the second, and 1/4 cup of ammonia into the third.

3) Pour three tablespoons of the grape-juice solution into each glass, and jiggle to mix. Then check the color.

Grape juice looks purple in liquids that are neutral—neither acid nor base. It turns light red when it reacts with an acid, and it turns dark green when it reacts with a base. Now you've identified the mystery base—the ammonia that turned the grape-juice indicator dark green.

Whip Up Some Blood

This *is* disgusting! Be sure to do it to creep out your friends and your parents. By the way, what you're going to make follows a recipe sometimes used to make blood for movie special effects.

You'll need:
- **clear corn syrup**
- **flour**
- **red food coloring**
- **cocoa powder**
- **water**
- **measuring spoons**
- **measuring cup**
- **spoon**
- **bowl**

Pour 1/4 cup of corn syrup into the bowl. Add two table-spoons of flour and stir until well mixed. Add more flour as needed to make the mixture thick but still able to drip off the spoon. Add eight drops of red food coloring or enough to make the mixture bright red. Then add 1/4 teaspoon of cocoa powder or just enough to make the fake blood reddish brown.

Actors would have some of this mixture in a gelatin capsule in their mouth so they could bite it and let the fake blood ooze out. Or they would have a capsule packed into a nostril so a tap could break it and make their nose drip fake blood.

Paint a little of your fake blood onto the corner of your mouth or below one nostril to see how this special effect looks.

Did you ever wonder why your body has blood? This fluid is like a railroad train, traveling around and around, carrying food and water and oxygen to all of the cells that make up your body. The part of your blood that makes it look red are the red cells. These are shaped something like Frisbees. The fluid part of the blood, called *plasma*, is clear, but blood looks red because there are so many red blood cells—about 2.5 trillion per pint. To figure out how much blood you have, use this formula supplied by Arlen Grey at the Egleston Children's Hospital Family Library in Atlanta. Children have about sixty-seven to seventy-five milliliters of blood per kilogram of body weight. So use seventy milliliters as an average and multiply this number times your weight in kilograms. If your scale measures only in pounds, multiply the number on the scale by 0.4536 to convert to kilograms.

The coloring material that gives red cells their special hue is a pigment called *heme*, which contains iron. If you've ever seen a rusty nail, you've probably noticed that's it's reddish—kind of like dried blood. The heme pigment combines with a kind of protein in your body called *globin* to form hemoglobin. This substance has a natural attraction to oxygen, one of the gases in the air. So as the blood comes in contact with air in the lungs, it attaches to oxygen and carries this gas along to the cells.

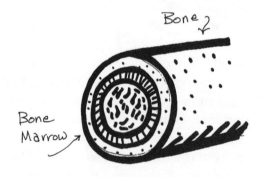

Bone

Bone Marrow

Your body gets the iron-rich heme it needs from two sources: old red blood cells that are being broken down and iron-rich foods you eat, such as liver, eggs, green leafy vegetables, and whole-grain bread. Red blood cells are constantly being knocked together and bumping into the walls of *arteries* (tubes that carry blood away from the heart) and *veins* (tubes that carry blood to the heart). So each red blood cell only lasts about a hundred days. Then broken-down ones are removed by the liver and spleen. But don't worry about running out of red blood cells. In normal healthy bodies, a special material called *red bone marrow* is found inside the vertebrae, the sternum, the ribs, the clavicle, the scapula, and in parts of the femur and humerus. Red bone marrow produces red blood cells.

Amy Harris, medical technologist at the Atlanta chapter of the American Red Cross, explained that people are categorized as having one of four different blood types: A, B, AB, and O, with O being the most common, A second, B third, and AB rarest. What blood types really indicate is that the red blood cells produce special proteins called *antigens* inside the cells. These proteins then push through the cell membranes or walls. And they attract special sugars that attach to the outside of the red blood cell. For example, people with type A blood have two kinds of sugars attached to each red blood cell—*L-sucose* and *N-acetyl-galactosamine*. Whatever particular type of blood you have was directly inherited from your parents.

In addition to the antigens that determine these blood types, there is another antigen called the *RH* antigen. It's named RH after the rhesus monkey in which researchers first observed this antigen. People who have this RH antigen on their red blood cells are said to be RH positive. Those who don't are said to be RH negative. It's more common for people to be RH positive than negative. The RH type is generally listed with the ABO type, so, for example, someone is said to be AB negative or O positive.

Knowing a person's RH blood type as well as his or her ABO blood type is important in case the person needs a transfusion of blood to make up for significant blood loss. If the body recognizes the transfused blood as "foreign," the red cells are likely to clump together. Then they won't function properly. The red blood cells may also burst, dumping hemoglobin into the bloodstream. Then the kidneys, unable to handle processing all the hemoglobin, are likely to shut down. Other body systems may also fail, and the person could die.

The blood flowing away from the heart and lungs through arteries is bright red. When hemoglobin is in contact with oxygen, the way it is inside arteries, it appears bright red. The blood moving through veins on its way back to the heart is sometimes said to be blue, but it's really dark, purplish red. That's the color hemoglobin looks when there's very little oxygen present. The blood's just being in contact with the air reactivates the hemoglobin, though. So when you have a cut that bleeds, the blood flowing out onto the skin always looks bright red.

Did You Know that There Are Real Bloodsuckers?

Vampire bats (*Desmodus rotundus*) are probably the best-known bloodsuckers. This small bat is only about eight centimeters (three inches) long. But small is better when you're trying to sneak up on a sleeping prey animal—most often cows. The bat searches for an animal, preferably a female or a calf, on the edge of the herd. The cow also has to be lying down in such a way that a good vein will be exposed. When the vampire bat spots a likely prey animal, it lands and hops over to it. It may then take as long as twenty minutes before the bat can enjoy its blood meal. First the bat uses its *cheek teeth*—a vampire bat's molars—to shave away the victim's hair. Unlike your molars, the bat's cheek teeth have sharp points. Next, it licks and licks the shaved area, creating a puddle of saliva that contains an *anticoagulant*, or special chemical that prevents blood from clotting. Finally, it uses its two sharp incisors to puncture the vein and start the blood flow. Then the bat laps up the blood with its tongue. If the bat has rabies or a kind of blood parasite called a *trypanosome*, these infections are transmitted to the cow through the bat's saliva.

Vampire bats can cause their prey to lose a lot of blood, but not from just that one bite. A bat only consumes about two tablespoonfuls of blood before it quits eating. However, vampire bats rarely go out to dinner alone. Females have young who go along and eat after the mothers finish. Older offspring come along and wait their turn. Then, because it's easier to reopen a wound than to create a new one, the bat will try to return to the same cow the next night.

While thinking about vampire bats can be spooky fun, you don't need to worry about being attacked. Vampire bats live in Central and South America, and even in these countries people rarely sleep outdoors in the open where they could become prey.

Leeches (members of the Hirudinea family) are

bloodsuckers, too. Most live in water and some get to be as much as forty-two centimeters (about seventeen inches) long. These worms have a suction-type disc at each end of their body to let them grab onto their victim. The disc at the front surrounds the mouth. And leeches have sharp teeth to slice their victim's skin. They, like the vampire bat, also produce an anticoagulant. A leech can suck as much as three times its weight in blood. It then takes as long as several months to digest its food before it needs to eat again.

For centuries leeches were used by doctors to treat sick people. It was believed that fevers and certain other diseases were the result of an excess of blood in the body. So doctors carried leeches in bottles and attached them to a sick patient. If you think that's disgusting, you won't want to read on.

Today doctors have found a new use for leeches. In some cases, leeches are considered to be the best way to remove extra blood from swollen sensitive tissue, such as around the eyes, after surgery or after a skin transplant.

Have You Got Alektorophobia?

Do you get scared sometimes? That's normal, but some people have an intense, irrational fear of something—even something as harmless as a book. Such irrational fears have names and they all end in *phobia*, which means "fear of." Check out this list of phobias to see if just thinking about any of these makes shivers run down your spine. Then take a survey to find out how many people are scared of one or more of these things. Be sure to follow the directions for conducting a scientifically accurate survey.

If you're scared of . . .	you're said to have . . .
books	bibliophobia
cemeteries	coimetrophobia
chickens	alektorophobia
clouds	nephophobia
dolls	pedophobia
flowers	anthophobia
going to school	scolionophobia

laughter	geliophobia
mirrors	catoptrophobia
money (especially germs on it)	chrematophobia
peanut butter sticking to the roof of your mouth	arachibutyrophobia
spiders	arachnophobia
teeth	odonophobia
taking tests	testophobia
the number 13	triskaidekaphobia
vegetables	lachanophobia

Now it's time to find out what is most likely to scare people. Surveys are a great way to check up on all sorts of things. First you need to select your survey group. For the very best results, you should try to talk to a hundred people. And those

people should be chosen at random to include a mix of men and women or boys and girls of different ages and backgrounds. Of course, it isn't always possible to survey such a large group of people, but to make it easier to analyze the results, always try to check an even number, such as ten, twenty, thirty, and so forth.

Copy the list of things that may cause phobias. Have people look at it, telling you anything that makes them scared just to think about it—especially if it's something that has always frightened them. After you conduct your survey, sort the responses by categories. For example, identify how many people are scared silly by spiders, how many are terrified of the number 13, and so forth.

A bar graph is a good way to display the results of your survey. On a sheet of paper, draw columns of identical blocks, side by side, for each of the phobias selected. Label the columns "bibliophobia," and so forth. Next, color in one block in each column to represent one person who admitted to having that particular phobia. Or if you survey a large number of people, one block could represent two people.

Now, at a glance, your graph will let you analyze the results of the survey. What seems to frighten the most people? So many people have a fear of the number 13 that many office buildings and large hotels don't have a thirteenth floor.

By the way, if you've got alektorophobia, would you be more likely to panic at the sight of a chicken or a spider?

Send a Spooky Message

Here's a chance to send a message that disappears after you write it. Then nobody can read it unless he or she knows the secret science of how to make the words visible again. So be sure the person to whom you're sending the message knows the secret.

You'll need:
- **lemon juice**
- **plain white paper**
- **a cotton-tipped swab or a paintbrush**

To write your message, dip the swab or brush into the lemon juice and paint the letters on the paper. Keep redipping so the swab or brush is wet. You should be able to see the letters clearly while they're wet. Work quickly, however, because the letters will disappear as they dry. Once the paper is completely dry, mail it to your friend.

To reveal the secret writing, your friend will need to heat the paper. This can be done by ironing the paper. Or your friend can wear oven mitts and move the paper slowly back and forth through the hot air rising above a lightbulb. Remember to caution your friend not to let the paper touch the hot lightbulb.

Wayne Robbins, director of the Research Services Division at the Institute of Paper Science and Technology, explained the science that makes this apparent magic work. The lemon juice attacks the paper fibers, breaking them down. This breaking-down process normally happens to paper because the wood fibers also contain acid. That's why over time white paper will turn yellow and then brown. The acid in the lemon juice speeds up this process, and when the paper is heated, the process happens even faster.

Is there anything else that you could use to write invisible messages that appear when heated? You'll probably think of other solutions to try, but here are a few to get you started: milk, onion juice, and tea. Once you've decided what to try, check your ideas with an adult to be sure what you plan to test is safe for you.

There's a Ghost in a Bottle!

Shh. Listen. There's a ghost in that bottle. You can hear it. It's about to escape. Watch out!

*Note: Try this activity and you'll be able to see the ghost escape. Then read on to find out what really happens.

You'll need:
- **empty plastic film container with a snap-on lid (free at stores that handle film processing)**
- **Alka-Seltzer tablet**
- **measuring spoons**
- **water**
- **safety goggles**

To stay safe, do this activity outdoors and wear your safety goggles. Put a teaspoon of water in the plastic film container. Set the can on the ground or sidewalk. Unwrap the tablet and break off about a fourth of it. Drop this fourth into the film container, snap on the lid, and quickly back away about one meter (three feet).

You may or may not hear any sounds coming from inside the container, but you'll quickly see the ghost escape. At least you'll see the lid shoot into the air.

Did a ghost really escape from the container? No! When Alka-Seltzer dissolves in water, it releases carbon dioxide gas—the same gas that makes soda pop fizz and that you breathe out. There is already air inside the container, so adding carbon dioxide gas is like pouring more water into a glass full of water. Eventually the container can't hold any more, and the pressure becomes so great the cap blasts off. Then the carbon dioxide gas—not a ghost—escapes into the air.

Just a little does a lot!

Uh-oh, Your Bones Are Showing!

Brace yourself for a scary peek at your interior. You're about to see your own bones and blood vessels.

All you need is a flashlight and someplace dark like the outdoors at night or inside a closet. Switch on the flashlight and place one hand, palm down, over the flashlight's beam. What you see will depend partly on your skin color and the thickness of your hand. But your hand should have a reddish glow. This color is partly from the blood in your skin and also from your muscles. Blood carries food and oxygen to all parts of your body. Muscles move your bones. Can you see dark lines in your hand? These are shadows of blood vessels and bones. The blood vessels appear like a network spreading from your wrist to your fingers. The bones are solid shapes.

All the bones in your body form your skeleton, the framework that supports you. Your bones grow longer as you grow taller, so they are always just the right size for you.

Now try shining the flashlight's beam through your arm. You may not see anything here because there is more muscle to block the light. Try shining the light through your toes. Do you see any bone shadows now?

Check Out Strange
Blinking Lights in the Night

Go outside on a warm, summer evening and you're likely to see some tiny lights blinking on and off. Are these alien tourists? Or could they be ghost eyes winking?

No, they're fireflies. With a penlight flashlight you can communicate with these little flashers. If you're good enough at mimicking the blinking pattern, you may even get a firefly to come to you.

Fireflies blink to attract a mate. During the daytime, both male and female fireflies stay hidden under leaves or bits of bark. But once it's dusk, they begin to blink. Just as different birds have different songs, different kinds of fireflies blink in their own distinct pattern.

If you live in the eastern United States, the most common firefly is *Photinus pyralis*, which is found from New York through Florida and west to Kansas. The males of this kind of firefly usually fly while they signal to females waiting on leaves or blades of grass near the ground. So to attract a Photinus male, sit on the grass in the dark and watch. When you see a flashing firefly, pay close attention to how many times it flashes and how long each flash lasts. The male will repeat his glowing message about every six seconds, so you'll get more than one chance to identify the pattern. If you're not sure what the blinking pattern was, try this one: Switch the light on and off, switch it on and count "one thousand one" before switching it off, and then quickly switch it on and off again. Can you spot a firefly mimicking *your* light pattern?

When you're mimicking a pattern, hold your penlight near the ground and count "one thousand one, one thousand two," before returning the flashing signal. A female usually pauses briefly before responding. If you are lucky enough to get a male to approach where you're sitting, tip your light down. The female Photinus dims her light as the male flies closer. But don't actually catch any fireflies; let them find a mate so they can produce more fireflies.

Are you wondering how the fireflies produce their nightlights? This flash results from a chemical reaction that happens inside special cells called *photocytes* in the firefly's tail end. These lie just beneath a protective transparent layer, the *cuticle*. The chemical *luciferin* is produced inside the photocytes along with an enzyme called *luciferase*. When the luciferase reacts with the luciferin in the presence of oxygen, the result is energy released in the form of a flash of light. Since this whole reaction is triggered by a nerve impulse, the light flashes are controlled, producing some long and some shorter flashes—a signal. Unlike fire or even a lightbulb, a firefly's light generates only a tiny amount of heat.

Fast Facts About Fireflies

*Fireflies aren't flies at all. They're beetles. There are about two thousand different kinds of fireflies in the world.

*Female *Photurus* fireflies are able to mimic the patterns of a number of different kinds of fireflies. When a male of a different species comes close, a female Photurus grabs him. Then she eats him!

*In Thailand, where the foliage is very thick, male *Pteroptyx malaccae* fireflies gather together on certain trees along riverbanks. Groups flash in unison so females will be able to find them. Sometimes the whole tree will appear to be flashing at once.

Invasion of the Creepy, Crawly Body Beasties

All of these skin-tunneling, bloodsucking, body-munching critters are real. They're *parasites*, living creatures that make their home on the bodies of other living things—like you. And they usually harm their host in the process. So once you figure which of the facts about these body invaders *is* true, watch out! Your body could have unwelcome guests.

1. *Loa loa* worms like to live in human tissue and burrow along just under the skin, eating as they go, at a rate of about 1.5 centimeters (half an inch) a minute. True or False.

2. There are probably wormlike creatures called *mites* living at the base of your eyelashes. True or False.

3. *Screwworm* eggs are carried in raindrops. When the eggs land on skin, they hatch and the baby worms twist around and around, screwing themselves into their host. True or False.

4. You can get *pinworms* by chewing your fingernails. True or False.

5. Fleas never bite people, only dogs and cats. True or False.

Solutions:

1. TRUE. Loa loa worms belong to a group of worms called filarial worms that often plague people who live in tropical places, like West Africa and Central America—especially places with poor sanitation. Loa loa worms spread when young worms get into the bloodstream and are sucked up by a biting mango fly (*Chrysops*). When this fly then bites someone else, the young worms get into the wound and settle into their new host. The adults are wanderers, traveling around the host's body. Sometimes they can even be seen as a ripple, wiggling through the white of a person's eye.

2. TRUE. *Demodex folluculorum* is so common there's better than a 50 percent chance there's one or more living at the base of your eyelashes. Most mites look like spiders and have eight legs, but Demodex's belly is so big and its legs are so little it looks and wiggles like a worm. But don't panic. Demodex is a parasite, but it lives off dead cells and only rarely causes any symptoms. Don't try scrubbing to get rid of Demodex, either. This body beastie is found more often on clean, healthy skin than on dirty, diseased skin.

3. FALSE. Screwworm is actually the nickname given to the young of a large number of flies, including *Phaenicia sericata*. Phaenicia adults are attracted by wounds or sores oozing pus. They lay their eggs in the wound, and the young, called *maggots*, eat the dead flesh. Because maggots' wastes tend to kill the bacteria

in the wound, doctors sometimes placed them on wounds on purpose. Then scientists learned that the maggots would attack living tissue as soon as the dead tissue was eaten up.

4. TRUE. Pinworms (*Enterobius vermicularis*) are very contagious because the worms leave their host and explode, spraying tiny eggs into the air. Then touching clothes, furniture—anything—transfers the eggs to a person's hands, where the eggs most often lodge under fingernails. Then chewing the nails introduces the eggs into the body. Inside the body, the eggs hatch and the young quickly develop. Adult worms, which are only about two to thirteen millimeters long (a tiny fraction of an inch), live in the intestines and appendix. At night, they migrate out the anus to deposit eggs. This movement causes intense itching, and in scratching, the host picks up eggs again. Then guess what happens if this person bites his or her nails.

5. FALSE. Fleas do bite people. In the process of sucking blood, some germs, if there are any present in the digestive track of the flea, are likely to be regurgitated. The flea is usually unaffected by the germs in its gut, but the person gets sick. Since fleas may also go on to bite other people, the disease can quickly spread until lots of people are sick all at once. When that happens, it's called an *epidemic*. Scientists believe fleabites helped spread the bubonic plague that killed some twenty-five million people—one-fourth of the population of Europe—during the fourteenth century.

Make Your Own Strange Cave Formations

Caves, especially those that form in limestone rock formations, can be spooky places with lots of strangely shaped formations called *stalactites* and *stalagmites*. Stalactites have their base on the cave ceiling; stalagmites on the floor. So how do stalactites and stalagmites form? Follow these directions to find out.

You'll need:
- **2 juice glasses or plastic cups**
- **Epsom salts**
- **water**
- **spoon**
- **measuring cup**
- **sturdy paper plate**
- **40 centimeters of yarn**

Fill one glass two-thirds full of hot water. Pour in eight tablespoons of Epsom salts, stirring until the crystals are dissolved. Pour half of this solution into the other glass. Set one glass on either side of the plate. Submerge the yarn in one glass. Pull the yarn out slowly, squeezing out excess liquid with your fingers. Stretch the yarn between the two glasses, letting it droop over the plate but not touching it. If the ends of the yarn float up from inside the glass, weight them down with pebbles. Check the plate after fifteen minutes.

You'll discover that some of the salty solution flowed through the yarn and dripped onto the plate. Remove the yarn. Let the plate set overnight. In the morning examine the plate closely. You should see and feel some salt deposited where the water from the salty solution dripped and the water *evaporated*, or moved into the air. This process built up only a thin layer of salt, but cave formations form layer upon layer over many years. The layers that build up from drips that land on the cave floor form stalagmites. (Use the *g* in the middle of this word to remind yourself it's the name of formations that develop from the ground up.) The icicle-like formations that build up layer by layer from the ceiling down are called stalactites. (Use the *c* in the middle of this word to remind yourself it's the name of formations that develop from the ceiling down.)

Stalactites and stalagmites are made up of a chemical called *calcium carbonate*, which forms when water seeps down through limestone rock and through tiny cracks in the ceiling of a cave. A little of the calcium carbonate is deposited in a ring around the edge of a water drop. This material builds up—drop after drop—over hundreds of years. Because the calcium carbonate creates a crust around the drop of water, stalactites are hollow. Stalagmites form from drops that land on the cave floor, depositing a layer of calcium carbonate that builds up layer upon layer over hundreds of years. So stalagmites usually aren't hollow.

Some people who visit caves break off pieces of stalactites or stalagmites to take home as souvenirs. Why is this a bad thing to do?

Stalactites

Stalagmites

"You can remember: 'Stalactites stick tight to the ceiling!'"

Make Things that Go Screech in the Night!

Want to produce sounds spooky enough to give you and your friends goose bumps? You can with a little help from science. And to make this activity especially effective, do it in the dark.

You'll need:
- **orange-juice can (sides can be cardboard if the bottom is metal)**
- **large coffee can**
- **any other can that's metal or has a metal bottom**
- **nail**
- **hammer**
- **safety goggles**
- **sturdy cotton packaging twine**
- **1 paper clip per can**
- **scissors**
- **masking tape**
- **a piece of clean sponge (about 2.5 centimeters/ 1 inch square)**

This activity requires punching a hole in a metal can, so work with an adult partner and follow the directions carefully, to stay safe.

The cans need to be clean and empty with the tops

completely removed. Have your adult partner use the nail and hammer to punch a hole through the center bottom of each can. The hole should be just big enough for the twine to slip through.

Next, cut a piece of twine about forty centimeters long for each can. Thread one piece of twine through the inside of each can. Tie the end of the twine that pokes through the metal-can bottom to a paper clip. Pull the twine so the paper clip is resting on the can bottom and tape it in place.

Now wet the sponge and squeeze out the water. To make your can squeal, hold the can in one hand. With your other hand, pinch the sponge against the string and give it a jerk. This makes the metal-can bottom vibrate, which in turn creates waves of air that pass through a short canal and bump into your eardrum.

Then three tiny bones inside your middle ear wiggle, and this wiggling triggers special cells inside your inner ear to send messages to your brain. When your brain puts together these messages, you hear the spooky noises. Of course, this process happens almost instantly.

You can make different spooky sounds by pulling the damp sponge down the string in short jerks or in one long slide. The can acts like

an amplifier, making the sounds louder.

If you wanted to make an even deeper sound, would you need a can that's bigger or smaller than the cans you used? To help you decide, compare the sounds made by your biggest and smallest cans.

Did you guess that you'd need a bigger can? The taller the column of vibrating air the deeper the sound that's produced. Whether a sound is high or low is called its *pitch*.

More Spooky Sounds

Can you think of some other things you could make vibrate to produce spooky sounds? You'll probably think of lots more, but here are a few to get you started.

*A balloon—Blow it up and grip it between your legs so you can use both hands to stretch its neck. Then control how much air escapes.

*A comb—Hold it in one hand and run your fingernail back and forth across its teeth. To make the sound louder, touch one end of the comb to something that's wooden and hollow, such as a salad bowl or a door if it's hollow. That helps make the sound louder.

*A glass soda bottle—Put the rim next to your lower lip and blow a strong blast of air across the opening.

This Scavenger Hunt Will Make Chills Run Up and Down Your Spine!

Howls and squeaks, rustles and creaks—you're likely to hear lots of creepy noises outdoors. So get your friends together and divide up into groups. Each group will also need an adult partner. Then go outdoors, searching your neighborhood for sounds that fit each of the following categories. Take along a notepad to record where you heard the sound and what created it. If you have a tape recorder, take it along to capture the sounds and bring them home with you.

* A high-pitched sound
* A sound from somewhere overhead
* Sounds in a repeating rhythmic pattern
* A sound that might startle someone
* A sound that's irritating
* A sound made by an animal
* A sound created by the wind
* A sound made by something moving

Feel free to add other sounds to the list or to collect more than the ones required—especially sounds that are creepy and spooky.

A spooky favorite!

It's Alive!

Is there a poltergeist sealed inside the envelope? The word *poltergeist* comes from the German words *polter*, meaning a noise, and *geist*, meaning a spirit. So send a friend a letter with a noisy spirit tucked inside. And be sure to include a warning on the envelope: "Beware! Poltergeist inside."

You'll need:
- **2 rubber bands—each 2.5 to 5 centimeters (1 to 2 inches) long**
- **1 metal washer**
- **1 large metal paper clip**
- **1 small, sturdy envelope, such as a manila envelope that's about 4 centimeters by 13 centimeters (about 1.5 inches by 5 inches)**

Have an adult partner straighten the paper-clip wire and bend it into a V-shape with the ends spread about ten centimeters (four inches) apart. Have your partner also bend the ends of the wire into curls like the top of a question mark.

Next, thread one rubber band through the hole in the center of the washer. Pull the ends up so the washer is suspended by the rubber band. Then hook both ends of the rubber band over one curled end of the V. Repeat, looping the other rubber band through the metal washer and hooking it to the other curled end of the V.

Wind the washer so the entire length of the rubber bands become tightly twisted.

Holding the washer so the rubber bands won't unwind, slide the device into the envelope and seal the flap. Then mail it to someone you want to surprise. As soon as the envelope's flap is opened, the rubber bands are no longer trapped and can begin to unwind, returning to their original shape. The twisted rubber bands were storing *potential* energy. As the rubber bands untwist, the potential energy is transformed into *kinetic* or active energy. And this makes the washer spin. Since the washer is still at least partly inside the envelope, though, it bangs against the sides of the envelope each time it flips over. This action makes the paper vibrate. This in turn creates vibrations in the air that could make spooky noises.

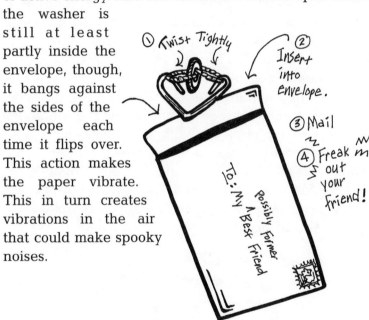

Did You Know that People Sometimes Were Buried Alive?

In the past it wasn't always possible to know if someone was dead or just in a coma. In fact, people were terrified of regaining consciousness only to discover themselves trapped inside a box underground. So during the early 1900s, the Society for the Prevention of Premature Burial was formed in America and in England. This group supported the development of techniques and equipment to help families know if their loved one was genuinely dead prior to burial. One of the procedures was to tie a string to the finger of the person being buried. The string passed through a hole in the coffin to a bell mounted on top of the grave. If the person wasn't actually dead and regained consciousness after being buried, it was possible to sound the alarm. Today there are machines to record when a person's heart has officially stopped beating so no one is buried unless it is certain that he or she is dead.

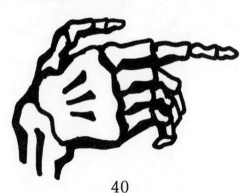

Who's Screaming?

Hang onto your hair because you're about to hear noises guaranteed to make it stand on end. Just follow the directions below.

You'll need:
- **chunk of dry ice (inexpensive and available from stores that sell ice and picnic supplies)**
- **oven mitts**
- **ice chest**
- **large metal spoon**
- **metal bowl**
- **hot tap water**

Work with an adult partner for this activity and follow the directions carefully, to stay safe.

Have your adult partner get the dry ice for you. You won't need much. If you're wondering why this frozen stuff is called *dry ice*, it's because it doesn't turn into a liquid when it melts. It changes directly into a gas and moves into the air. You may have already guessed that dry ice isn't frozen water. It's frozen carbon dioxide, the waste gas that people and animals breathe out. While water only has to be chilled to $0°C$ ($32°F$) to freeze, carbon dioxide must be chilled to $-78°C$ ($-108°F$) to turn to ice. And unlike water, it changes directly from a gas to a solid without ever being a liquid. Dry ice usually looks like snow, but it can be compressed into blocks. Average room temperature is enough to melt dry ice, and then it turns directly from a solid back to a gas. The process of changing directly from a solid to a gas is called *sublimation*.

You can take advantage of dry ice's sublimating to produce eerie noises that sound like screams. Fill the metal bowl half full with hot tap water. Put on the oven mitts and hold the bowl end of the spoon in the hot water for a few seconds. Then quickly press the hot spoon down hard against the block of dry ice.

Did the sound surprise you? When you pressed the hot spoon against the dry ice, you made the ice sublimate at that spot and change into a gas. The carbon dioxide gas then pushed up on the spoon as the gas escaped into the air, causing the metal spoon to vibrate. Like the vibrating can bottom, the vibrating spoon created air waves that sent messages to your brain that were interpreted as strange noises.

Reheat the spoon. This time, slide it across the dry ice as you press down. Repeat, rolling the spoon from side to side as you press it against the ice. You will be able to produce different creepy noises by using these different techniques. Do you think a teaspoon would make as loud a scream as the big spoon? Make a prediction based on what you've discovered so far. Then test your prediction.

I'm quivering and shivering!

Make Spooky Movie Special Effects

Now use what's left of the dry ice to create a special effect that's used to make movie settings look spooky.

You'll need:
- **flashlight**
- **a gallon of very warm water**
- **dry ice**

Work with an adult partner and follow the directions carefully, to stay safe.

Turn off the lights so the room is dark. Switch on the flashlight and pour some of the warm water over the dry ice. A thick fog will immediately form and roll over the sides of the ice chest. Shine the light at the fog and see what a ghostly effect this creates. Add more water and you'll see the fog sink to the floor and begin to spread out. The fog sinks instead of rises because cold air naturally sinks and the fog is much colder than the air around it. Can you think of a movie that was set in aswamp or a graveyard where there was thick moonlit fog? It probably looked a lot like this, and the effect may have been created just this way by using big chunks of dry ice.

Now blow on the fog or fan it. You'll create inter-
esting ghostly tendrils that rise and curl, adding to the
special effect. You usually can't see air move, but when
the fog moves with the air you can.

Did You Know that You Can't See Colors Well in the Dark?

What color is blood in the dark—red or nearly black? When light enters your eyes, it strikes a light-sensitive layer at the back of your eye called the *retina*. The retina is made up of two kinds of special cells: rods that help you see black and white, and cones that help you see color. Of course, you don't really see images until these cells send signals to your brain and your brain interprets them. But that happens almost instantly.

To function, the cones require daylight. The rods can function even in dim light, supplying outlines of objects but no color or detail. You can prove this to yourself by putting on something bright red and then going into a dark room. To be fair, you'll need to wait about five minutes to allow your eyes to adapt to the change in light. Then check out the red color. It will look gray to black, depending on the shade—but not red. This lack of color and detail is why even familiar things may look spooky at night.

The Truth About Sneaky Animals—Maybe

A special kind of praying mantis has body parts colored and shaped to look just like a flower. It stays perfectly still, waiting among blossoms for an unsuspecting insect to come close enough to catch. An orb web-weaving spider builds a strong, sticky web to trap flying insects. A goosefish is color camouflaged so that it can lie hidden on the seafloor. When a fish comes close, it opens its enormous mouth and gulps in a meal. Want to find out more fascinating facts about sneaky animals? Then don't miss this quiz.

1. A cat's eyes glow because they send out beams of light like flashlights so the cat can see in the dark. True or False.

2. All spiders spin silk webs to trap prey. True or False.

3. Many snakes are colored to let them hide—and wait. True or False.

4. The flashlight fish has pouches of glowing bacteria to light its way. True or False.

5. Some anglerfish have a glowing lure they can wiggle to attract prey. True or False.

SOLUTIONS:

1. FALSE. A cat's eyes appear to glow only because of a special reflective layer called the *tapetum lucidum*, which lies outside the light-sensitive layer at the back of the eye. Any light that passes through the light-sensitive layer strikes the reflective layer and is bounced back. In a dimly lit environment, this process gives the light-sensitive layer a second chance to detect any light and send signals to the brain. The reflection of bright light, such as a car's lights or even a flashlight, makes the cat's eyes look as if they're glowing.

2. FALSE. All spiders produce silk but some use other sneaky tricks to catch prey. One, *Scytodes*, often called the spitting spider, sprays a sticky gluelike substance, creating a net that anchors its prey to a leaf or twig. Another, that lives in sandy places in Africa, kills termites by brushing them with its front legs. This touch spreads a powerful toxin that quickly immobilizes the termite.

3. TRUE. Not all snakes have camouflage coloring but those that do blend in perfectly. Some are colored to look like dry fallen leaves on the ground. Others that

crawl along branches in tree-tops are bright green. Still others that live in the desert blend in perfectly with the sand. Holding very still, these sneaky hunters wait until their prey comes close. Then they strike.

4. TRUE. Flashlight fish, which range in length from eight to thirty centimeters (about three to eight inches) have a bean-shaped pouch below each eye. The pouches contain bacteria that are the fish's partners. The flashlight fish supplies the bacteria with food and oxygen through blood vessels that extend into the pouches. In return, the bacteria glow, letting the fish attract prey and confuse enemies by swimming in a zigzag path while blinking. The bacteria don't flash. Some types of flashlight fish have a sort of eyelid they can pull up over the glowing pouches to block the light. Others have special muscles that rotate the pouches downward like changing the direction of a car's head-light beams.

5. TRUE. Some anglerfish have a thin filament-like rod attached to their heads. The tip of this is a fleshy bulb that glows. By wiggling this bulb and then laying it back in a groove on its head, the anglerfish draws prey close. Lying still with its huge mouth open, the angler-fish waits until its prey is close. Then it lunges and gulps in its dinner.

Be a Shadow Stalker

People have always been spooked by creepy shadows in the moonlight. Long ago some people believed there were monstrous creatures called ghouls who went into graveyards at night, dug up dead bodies, and ate them. Supposedly ghouls sometimes also snatched living people if they were caught out at night. So when people saw ghastly-looking shadows in the moonlight, they were suspicious that these were ghouls.

Luckily, there aren't such things as ghouls, but shadows can look creepy at night. The next time there's a full moon and no clouds to block the light, go shadow hunting outdoors with an adult partner. Go right after it first gets completely dark. Take along a tape measure, a flashlight to use while recording data, and a copy of the chart below. Also take along strips of cloth to mark the objects that cast each shadow you measure. Return two hours later to remeasure each shadow's length.

Shadow	Shadow's Length at Dark	Shadow's Length 2 Hours Later
Shortest		
Longest		
Spookiest-looking		
Roundest-looking		

(Note: No fair measuring shadows cast by any source other than moonlight, such as street lights, flashlights, or building lights.)

Because light travels in straight lines, a shadow ends where the first light rays clear the top of the object. When the light source is nearly straight over the top of the object, the first rays will strike near the object's base. When it's lower, the first light rays clearing the object fall farther away. So you should discover that shadows appear longer just after dark, when the moon is near the horizon. Later, when the moon appears higher in the sky, the shadow should look shorter.

But to be sure of your results, you should do what scientists do. They always repeat a test at least three times to be sure the results are what's likely to happen every time. So, if possible, repeat this test on two more nights while the moon is still nearly full. You can probably guess now why you weren't allowed to measure shadows cast by any light source other than the moon. Light sources, like street lights, produce shadows that remain the same length because the sources don't change position.

Things that Go Bloom in the Dark

You may be surprised to learn that some flowers only bloom at night. Here are some that you can plant in a garden or even in a container on a balcony so you can watch them bloom by moonlight.

*Night-flowering jasmine (*Cestrum nocturnum*). A shrub native to the West Indies, it has cream-colored tubular flowers. It likes partial to full sun during the day, and if you live where it gets below 10°C (50°F), it will need to be grown in a pot that can be brought indoors during cold weather. This plant's special gift is that after sunset the flowers give off a wonderful fragrance.

*Moonflower (*Ipomoea alba)* is a climbing vine native to tropical America that produces white blooms—often as much as fifteen centimeters (about six inches) wide. Each bloom lasts only one night before wilting. Moon-flowers can be started from seed, and soaking the seeds overnight helps them sprout faster.

*One type of night-blooming cereus (*Hylocereus undatus*) is the star of any garden. It's actually a type of cactus native to Brazil and prefers being in a pot with sandy, fertile soil to being in the ground. Each of its blooms lasts only one night. The bud begins to unwrap about 9 P.M., one petal curling back at a time. Fully opened, the flower may be as much as thirty centimeters (about eleven inches) across. At daybreak the blossoms rapidly wilt.

Wonder why any flowers would bloom at night? The reason is that they depend on bats or night-flying insects to carry, from one plant to another, the pollen they need to produce seeds. Night bloomers are often white because colors are not usually visible at night. And they produce a strong scent to attract the night pollinators.

Spooky Zooky!

Are There Wicked Plants?

Is it possible for a plant to defend itself from animals that might want to eat its leaves? Could some plants actually set traps to catch animals and then digest them? To find the answers to these plant questions and more, take this quiz.

1. *Sorghum*, or Indian millet, is an important grain crop in many tropical countries, but its leaves are deadly. True or False.

2. The sharp curved thorns on the stems of roses are there only to discourage animals that might eat the plant's leaves. True or False.

3. Anyone who touches poison ivy will break out in an itchy rash. True or False.

4. *Puffballs* shoot clouds of poisonous gas into the air. True or False.

5. The cobra lily (*Darlingtonia californica*), which grows in northern California and southern Oregon in the United States, got its name because it produces a poison as deadly as cobra venom. True or False.

SOLUTIONS:
1. TRUE. A number of plants, like sorghum, have devel-

oped a natural protection against animals that eat leaves. The poison in sorghum leaves is a kind of cyanide. When the leaves are chewed, the cyanide is released, affecting the animal's breathing—often killing it.

2. FALSE. Rose thorns also help the plant grip surfaces and climb. In fact, the thorns are only superficially attached. Gently press on one, and it will break off without damaging the stem.

3. FALSE. People are rarely sensitive to poison ivy the first time they have contact with it. Only about half of the people who come in contact with this plant ever develop a sensitivity. The most common way to be exposed is by touching the leaves. These contain microscopic canals filled with an oily poison. The stems or roots are poisonous, too, but only if they are broken and the sap touches exposed skin. If you've touched poison ivy, washing immediately with strong soap and rinsing several times can remove the irritating oil.

4. FALSE. Sometimes called *smoke balls*, these mushrooms explode, producing a smoky cloud. This isn't poison gas, though. It's microscopic spores—the seedlike structures from which new puffballs grow. Puffballs are a type of mushroom, and the inside of the ball is a mass of threads and spores. When the spores are ready to be released, the surface of the ball dries and finally cracks open. Some giant puffballs may measure 1.8 meters (six feet) around. Imagine what a big explosion they produce!

5. FALSE. This plant is a killer, but it doesn't produce a poisonous substance. It belongs to a group of plants known as pitcher plants. Its trap is shaped like a cobra's hooded head. Beneath the hood is a lure of sweet nectar that attracts insects. But the surface of the plant inside its tubelike pitcher is slick. So insects seeking a nectar treat usually slip and drop into a little pool of water at the base of the tube. These plants grow where the soil is unable to supply all the minerals they need. So, instead, they trap insects, produce special juices that break down the insects' bodies, and then absorb this mineral-rich liquid.

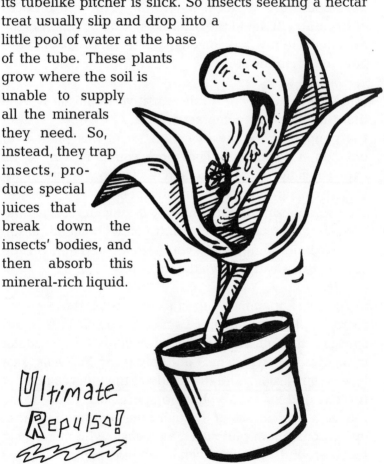

Ultimate
Repulsa!

Eek! There's a Ghost Peeking in the Window!

That's what you'll shriek when you create this optical illusion.

You'll need:
- **3 x 5 index card**
- **scissors**
- **hole punch**
- **colored pencils**
- **glue**
- **unlined white paper**
- **1 meter (a little more than 3 feet) of string or yarn**

Find a drinking glass that's just the right size, set it on the index card, and trace around it. Use this disk to trace two circles on the white paper. Cut out the paper circles.

Draw the outline of a window in the center of one paper circle. Place the other circle on top of this one so they line up exactly. Press the two circles against a window where sunlight will shine through the paper. Draw the outline of a spooky creature, so it appears in the center of the window. Keep the spooky creature simple because simple images work best for this illusion. Now keep the paper circles matched up, and punch small holes close to the top and bottom of the circles. Finish coloring the creature.

Glue the circle with the window to one side of the index card. Using the hole in the paper as a guide, punch holes through the index card. Use these holes to position the paper circle with the spooky creature on the opposite side of the disk. By being careful to line up the holes, the image of the creature should be exactly in the middle of the window, just as it was when you drew it. Thread one piece of string through each hole, bring the ends together, and knot.

Now have someone hold the two strings loosely stretched. Flip the circle over again and again, twisting the string. Stop so the empty window is facing you at

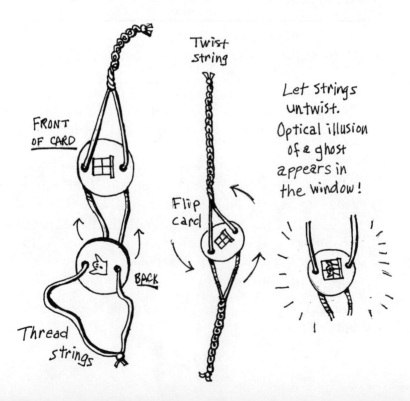

FRONT OF CARD

BACK

Thread strings

Twist string

Flip card

Let strings untwist. Optical illusion of a ghost appears in the window!

eye level. On your signal, release the disk and have your friend pull the ends of the strings apart. The string will untwist as it straightens, making the disk spin. Watch and you'll see the ghost appear to be looking through the window.

This spooky illusion takes advantage of the way your eyes work. At the very back of your eye there is a light-sensitive layer called the retina. When the light rays reflected from the object you're observing enter your eye and focus on the retina, a chemical change takes place in the cells the light strikes. This makes you perceive the image. And because the chemical change doesn't reverse instantly, you continue to see that image for a fraction of a second after what you were looking at is gone. This is called *persistence of vision*.

In 1834 William George Horner, a British watchmaker and noted mathematician, created a device called the *zoetrope* to take advantage of persistence of vision. The zoetrope contained a revolving drum covered with hand-drawn pictures. Each picture showed the same figure in a slightly different position. When the drum was set in motion and you were watching from just the right angle, the figure seemed to come alive and move through the positions. More than fifty years later, Émile Reynaud, a French inventor, added a projector to Horner's device. This new machine, which is called a *praxinoscope*, made it possible for a number of people to easily watch the animation at the same time. However, it wasn't until the movie camera was invented that the animation process became inexpensive enough to animate anything longer than the briefest action.

Bewitch an Egg

At one time it was believed that people suspected of being witches should be tossed into a lake. The theory was that a real witch would float. An egg, though, doesn't have to be bewitched to float. You can use science to create this spooky special effect.

You'll need:
- **quart jar**
- **table salt**
- **egg**
- **measuring spoons**
- **serving spoon**

Fill the jar two-thirds full of water. Gently ease the egg into the water. It should sink to the bottom. Lift out the egg. Add six tablespoons of table salt and stir while you slowly count to fifty. Ease the egg into the water again. The egg should now float. If it doesn't, remove the egg, stir in three more tablespoons of salt, and try again. Repeat until the egg floats.

If you've ever found it much easier to float in the ocean than in a freshwater lake or pool, you've experienced what's happening here. By adding salt to the water, you made it denser or thicker—dense enough to support the egg. How much salt would you need to add to suspend the egg halfway between the bottom of the jar and the surface of the water? Experiment to find out.

Take a Creepy Swamp Tour

You've undoubtedly seen pictures of swamps, marshes, and bogs as very wet and gloomy-looking places. Early settlers were afraid of swamps and imagined that all sorts of strange things lived there. Some unusual plants and animals do. Some wetlands are also very useful today. Want to find out more about these squishy places? Then take this quiz.

1. There are swamps all over the world. Some in the United States are protected by law against agricultural or commercial development. True or False.

2. The mysterious glow people sometimes see in swamps at night is really ghosts. True or False.

3. Some swamps produce a special material that can be dried and burned for fuel. True or False.

4. Swamps help prevent floods and droughts. True or False.

5. If you step into quicksand in a swamp, you'll be sucked under. True or False.

SOLUTIONS:
1. TRUE. So if you'd like to see a swamp for yourself, you and your family could visit one of these: Alakai

Swamp, Hawaii; Acadia National Park, Maine; Aransas National Wildlife Refuge, Texas; Bear River National Wildlife Refuge, Minnesota; Cape Cod National Seashore, Massachusetts; Four Holes Swamp, South Carolina; Glacier National Park, Montana; Grand Teton National Park, Wyoming; Great Cypress Swamp, Delaware; Isle Royale National Park, Michigan; Malheur National Wildlife Refuge, Oregon; Okefenokee National Wildlife Refuge, Georgia; and Reelfoot National Wildlife Refuge, Tennessee. The most unusual of these is Hawaii's Alakai Swamp because it's the only swamp located in a volcano crater.

2. FALSE. People have sometimes been tricked into thinking they saw ghosts in swamps. Certain types of toadstools and other *fungi*, plants that live off decaying plants and animals, glow in the dark. One type found in the United States is called the jack-o'-lantern fungus because its golden orange cap glows when it's mature. Certain bacteria that cause wood to rot also glow. And some gases given off as plants decay can seem to glow. But none of these are ghosts.

3. TRUE. This material is called *peat*. It forms in swamps when layers of plant material pile up and become waterlogged. The lower layers are compressed, and in time they carbonize. In places where other sources of fuel aren't readily available, people cut blocks of peat and let them dry—a process that can take as long as six weeks. Two of the largest sources of peat are the Dismal Swamp in Virginia and the Bog of Allen in Ireland. The Okefenokee Swamp in Georgia got its name because of

its floating peat islands. Although these looked like land, they were squishy and wobbled when someone walked on them. So the Seminole Indians called this swamp *Okefenokee,* meaning "land of shaking earth."

4. TRUE. The soil in swamps is often spongy. So it can soak up and trap more water than many surrounding areas during heavy rains. During long dry spells, the water retained in a swamp spreads out into the dry surrounding areas.

5. FALSE. Quicksand forms when a pool of water with a bottom that won't let the water soak in becomes partially filled with sand. Quicksand won't suck you under, but you'll sink as you displace the sandy mixture. An average man will usually sink about to his armpits. Making jerky movements makes the sandy mixture move away, letting you sink deeper before it packs in around you again. Of course, the best action is to avoid quicksand. But if you're ever caught, keep your legs still and move your arms in slow sweeping motions. Work to stretch out horizontally. You'll float and can slowly make swimming motions with your arms to reach solid ground. Then roll out of the quicksand.

Stretch out horizontally. Swim slowly!

DANGER! Quicksand

Roll onto shore.

What Happens to You When You're Scared?

It's a dark night, and you're all alone in the house. You hear footsteps downstairs. Naturally, you're scared. And when you're scared, your body responds in ways designed to get you ready to defend yourself or to run away. Here's what happens:

* Your heart starts to race. This is designed to pump more blood to your muscles so they're ready to fight or flee.

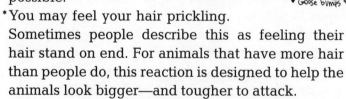

* Your pupils open wide, especially in dim light. This lets in more light to help you see as clearly as possible.
* You may feel your hair prickling. Sometimes people describe this as feeling their hair stand on end. For animals that have more hair than people do, this reaction is designed to help the animals look bigger—and tougher to attack.
* Your skin may feel sweaty. Your body starts to perspire to keep you cool even while you're being more active, defending yourself.

Why Are Dead Bodies Sometimes Called Stiffs?

It's a condition called *rigor mortis*, which literally means "stiffness of death."

You can experience what causes a body to stiffen after death by trying this harmless activity. Stand on one foot and lean against a wall to brace yourself. Now lift and bend the free leg at the knee. Next, stretch your leg out straight again. Repeat this action as rapidly as you can, until it becomes uncomfortable. Your leg will begin to feel stiff and you'll just naturally slow down. A weak acid, called *lactic acid*, is naturally produced when muscles are active. As an excess of this acid builds up in your leg, the muscles become temporarily rigid. Since you're alive, stopping this activity lets the blood carry away the excess acid, and your muscles recover.

After death, blood stops circulating and settles in the lowest parts of the body. Since oxygen is no longer reaching the muscles, a chemical reaction occurs that causes sugars that normally supply energy to break down in the muscles. Lactic acid forms and the muscles stiffen. Rigor mortis begins in the face and then extends to other parts of the body.

A dead body doesn't *stay* stiff, though. After about twelve hours, the muscles begin to relax as the effect of the acid goes away. Within forty-eight hours, the body is totally flexible once again.

Which Part of a Dead Body Rots First?

You can probably guess the answer if you think about what part of the body is responsible for breaking things down on a regular basis. If you guessed that the first part of the body to decompose (rot) is the belly, you're right. Bacteria that live in the intestines normally help break down food after it's eaten. After death, though, these same bacteria attack the walls of the intestines and move out into the body, causing tissues to liquefy. The first sign of this activity appears when the belly skin develops a greenish hue.

If the body is warm and wet, it rots much faster than if it's cold or dry. That's why dead bodies are kept in refrigerators at *mortuaries*, places where bodies are prepared for burial. Before refrigeration was common, undertakers had a special problem to handle. The decay process produces gas that can make the belly swell like a balloon. So the undertaker would have to pierce the body and hold a candle flame over the opening to burn the escaping gas. It wasn't uncommon for the gas to ignite, so there would be a flame flickering over the corpse's belly.

Even if decay happens quickly, though, the brain is one of the last soft parts to break down. That's because it's so well protected by the skull. Finally, though, only the body's hardest parts—bones and teeth—will be left.

Embalming—You Too Can Stop the Rot!

Today bodies aren't just buried, they're *embalmed.* It's a special process designed to keep bodies from decaying even after burial. The abdomen is cut, and a vacuum tube removes any body wastes and remaining undigested food. Next, a vein is cut and a tube inserted to drain out the blood. But most importantly, a special solution of chemicals, including formaldehyde, is pumped into the body through a major artery in the groin (where the leg joins the body), the neck, or under the arm.

Want to see how effective chemicals are at keeping flesh from rotting? Shari West, histology supervisor at the Emory School of Medicine, suggests the following activity.

You'll need:
- **2 slices of apple (preferably organic so the apple hasn't already been treated with a chemical preservative)**
- **2 clear plastic cups**
- **2 stainless-steel knives**
- **rubbing alcohol**

Rubbing alcohol is poisonous, so do not *eat the apple slices used in this experiment.*
Place one slice of apple in each cup. Pour rubbing

alcohol into one cup to cover the apple slice. Stick the knife into this apple slice to keep the slice submerged. Stick the other knife into the second apple slice so that both tests are identical in every way. Place the cups side by side in a warm place that's not likely to be exposed to direct sunlight. Let the cups sit overnight and check them in the morning. The apple slice that isn't in alcohol is likely to already have begun to rot. The one in alcohol is preserved because the alcohol prevents bacteria from attacking the apple.

Check it again after another day. How has the apple slice exposed to the air changed now? You should see a liquid in the bottom of the cup—that's a result of the decomposition or breakdown process. The apple slice in the alcohol should still look about the same.

Dump the rotting apple slice into the trash. You may want to keep the apple slice that's in alcohol for a few days longer to see for yourself that it's still not decomposing. But eventually, pour the alcohol down the drain and throw away the apple slice.

More than seventy years after the death of Vladimir Ilyich Lenin, leader of the 1917 Russian Revolution, embalmers continue the job of preserving his body which is on display in a glass coffin. So twice a week, the coffin is opened and Lenin's face and hands, the only skin showing, are wiped with embalming fluid to remove any bacterial growth.

Every eighteen months, Lenin gets a more thorough treatment. His clothes are removed and his body is immersed in a glass tub of chemicals, mostly glycerol and potassium acetate. This solution penetrates the skin and ensures that Lenin's body remains about 70 percent liquid—the same as a living person. Next, the body is hoisted onto a stretcher to drip dry, and everything that won't show under his clothes is bound with rubber bandages to seal in the liquid.

During World War II, Lenin's body was hidden in a special lab in the Ural Mountains. There this process was continued while keeping the body from being captured by the German army.

I'm a mad scientist!

Did You Know that Some People Just Burst into Flames?

Strange as this may sound, it's true, and dozens of cases have been reported over the years. For no reason anyone can explain, a person simply bursts into flames and within seconds the body is reduced to ashes. This is especially strange, since to cremate a human body requires it to be exposed to a temperature of more than 500°C (1,000°F) for at least ninety minutes.

Stranger still, spontaneous human combustion (SHC) doesn't cause anything else in the room to catch on fire. Occasionally even the person's clothing is unburned. Now that's SPOOKY!

Most Excellent Creepiness!

The Secrets of the Ice Man

Imagine going on a hike and suddenly discovering a dead body. That's what happened to Erika and Helmut Simon, a German couple who were hiking in the Ötztal Alps between Austria and Italy. The body they discovered was partly sticking out of a glacier, and at first everyone assumed it was just someone who had died during a hiking accident. Then, during the effort to dig the body out of the ice, someone found a knife with a wooden handle and a stone blade in the ice next to the body. There was also an ax with a copper head.

Just as a freezer keeps meat from rotting, the glacier had preserved this man's body since prehistoric time. In a way that no one yet understands, the body had also become strangely dried out like a mummy. The tools that were found with the body were proof this man lived long ago. The clothes, including a woven grass cape, were ancient, too. But the results of carbon-14 tests to find out just how old this ice man really was surprised everyone. He had been dead over five thousand years.

In case you're wondering how the carbon-14 test works, it's rather like sand trickling down through an hourglass. When an animal or a person is alive, the body builds up a supply of carbon 14 just as a natural by-product of breathing and eating. Then, after death, the carbon 14 starts to break down, and it decays at a rate that's as regular as the flowing sand. Scientists were able to determine the ice man's age by analyzing the amount of carbon 14 left in his bones. Being over five thousand years old makes the ice man the best-preserved example of ancient man ever discovered. But keeping him preserved so he won't decay is tricky. His skin is covered with surgical gauze. On top of that is a layer of crushed ice made from sterilized water. Next there's a plastic cover, more ice, and a final plastic wrap. Wrapped in this protective cocoon, the ice man is kept inside a high-tech freezer that stays at the same temperature as the glacier where he was entombed for so long. When researchers examine the body, they unwrap it carefully and place it in a chilled glass box filled with filtered, sterilized air. And they only keep it out of the freezer for thirty minutes at a time.